MONEY OF YOUR OWN

MONEY OF YOUR OWN

GRACE W. WEINSTEIN

E. P. DUTTON
NEW YORK

Library of Congress Cataloging in Publication Data

Weinstein, Grace W   Money of your own.

Includes index.

SUMMARY: Discusses the handling of money with emphasis on budgeting, learning to shop, uses of credit, saving, and attitudes towards money.

1. Finance, Personal—Juvenile literature.
2. Money—Juvenile literature. [1. Money.
2. Finance, Personal] I. Title.

HG179.W44 332'.024 77-3877 ISBN: 0-525-35145-0

Published in the United States by E. P. Dutton, a Division of Sequoia-Elsevier Publishing Company, Inc., New York

Published simultaneously in Canada by Clarke, Irwin & Company Limited, Toronto and Vancouver

Editor: Ann Troy   Designer: Nora Sheehan
Printed in the U.S.A.   First Edition   10 9 8 7 6 5 4 3 2 1

To Janet and Larry

CONTENTS

INTRODUCTION ix

1 | *Using Your Money*
Making Decisions 3
Budgets 9
Feelings About Money 16
Your Money's Worth 23
Shoplifting 47
Credit 50
Saving 62

2 | *Where Your Money Comes From*
Allowances 81
Earnings 89

INDEX 97

Introduction

Your friend Lynn always seems to have money to spend. Yet her allowance is no more than yours, and she doesn't work. How does she do it? Somehow, your money seems to disappear as fast as you get it.

Some people just seem to know instinctively how to manage money, how to spend wisely, how to have some left over. But it isn't instinct. It just takes the same good sense you apply to other areas of life—finding time for both hobbies and schoolwork, for instance, and doing well at both.

Money does come your way. You may get an allowance from your parents. You may be able to earn some money of your own. And you may have generous relatives who come through with cash on birthdays and holidays. What do you do with that money? What would you like to do?

You may enjoy ice-skating. You may be a movie freak. Perhaps books are your passion. Or clothes. Or chocolate-marshmallow ice-cream sundaes. Whatever your particular joy in life, it probably costs money. But there are ways to make the most of what you have. . . . This book is designed to help.

1 USING YOUR MONEY

MAKING DECISIONS

"I made $3.50 baby-sitting and then I spent it all going bowling. I wish I had saved some so I could get a record next week."

Sound familiar? You may have bought a record, then wanted to go to a movie. Or gone to a movie and missed the high school football game. Perhaps you simply bought a candy bar, then wished for an ice-cream cone. We all, young people and adults alike, sometimes have second thoughts, sometimes wish we hadn't done one thing with our money so that we might do something else. The need for second thoughts, however, can be minimized with a little thinking ahead.

No matter how little or how much money you have, no matter whether it comes from an allowance or from earnings or from gifts, money must be allocated. Somewhere along the way, every individual has to make personal decisions about what is most important, what comes first. If you don't stop to think about what you're doing with your money, it probably just disappears. The full pocket of Sunday becomes the empty pocket of Wednesday . . . with half the week stretching forlornly ahead. And the adequate allowance of September, when the school year begins, may seem completely inadequate by December, if you haven't planned ahead.

Your decisions about spending are personal decisions; they center on what is most important to *you*. And, because you change and your interests change, your spending decisions and priorities change too. What is most important in sixth grade may not seem very important at all in eighth; what is important one week may not even seem important the next week. Don't worry about changing your mind; it would be wrong to stay the same as circumstances change. But planning helps you do what is important to you at any particular time. Planning cuts down on impulse spending, the kind of spending so often regretted. Planning puts you in control.

The key to being in control, to having the money you want when you want it, is making decisions. Making decisions about money includes two things:

- Determining your short-term goals and your long-term goals.
- Deciding what is a necessity and what is a luxury.

GOALS

You may receive an allowance from your parents on a weekly basis. Or you may be given money as you need it. In any case, a week is a reasonable span of time for short-term spending decisions. Within the span of a week, you may spend money, or think about spending money, on a wide variety of things: school lunches and after-school snacks, a comic book or a magazine or notebook paper, a movie or hobby equipment or the latest record. You may buy a ticket to a school football game or concert. You may purchase a birthday gift. You may do all or some or none of these things in a given week. But these are the things that most young people spend their money on.

You may also think about things you would like to do in the future: to buy a special game or a pair of skates, to take a trip, or save for special schooling. Many young people put aside some money regularly toward such long-range goals.

Think about *your* long-term goals, the things you want which may cost more money than you have in a given week and the things which you know will come along at a later time. You might, for instance, want to get the brand of sneakers that all your friends are wearing. Your parents may see no reason to buy another pair of sneakers, since you already have a serviceable pair. But you know it's important to have that particular brand, and you are willing to save your money until you can buy them for yourself.

You may have a summer bicycle trip as a long-term goal. You may want a fine microscope to pursue an interest in science. Or you may be looking ahead to the inevitable holiday season, and all the gifts you will want to buy for family and friends. Unless you can expect a sudden new source of income before each of these occasions, some long-term planning is in order.

Think about the things you want to have right away and the things you want to have in the long run. Balance one against the other. Will today's candy bar provide as much enjoyment as the record you can buy if you skip candy bars for a few weeks? Put another way, do you want that ten-speed bike badly enough to pass up all the current movies? Which will give you the most pleasure over a longer period of time?

LUXURIES AND NECESSITIES

In balancing short-term interests and long-range goals, you also have to think about the difference between necessities and luxuries. A necessity, of course, is anything you absolutely have to have. A luxury is something you would like to have but can do without. That definition means that one person's necessity is another person's luxury. You may absolutely have to have those sneakers; they may be so essential to you that you are willing to do without ice-cream sodas and comic books for a few weeks or months.

Your best friend, on the other hand, might find the pleasures of after-school snacks more important than fashionable footwear. Some things are necessities at one time, luxuries at another. Records of the newest hit tunes may seem something you absolutely have to have, but you really could do without them if you had to. In fact, if you wait, you may no longer want them. Fashions change; so do your interests.

Most long-range purchases fall into the luxury or optional category, but some are absolutely essential. The same item may be both. If you need a good bicycle for a summer hosteling trip, the trip may be important to you but the need is optional. If you need a good bicycle before you can deliver papers or get to a baby-sitting job, then the purchase is essential.

Family birthdays are another mixture, both optional and necessary to observe. You don't have to buy an elaborately expensive present—but you don't want to hurt mother's feelings by letting her birthday pass without some remembrance. Birthdays, however, come but once a year, making it possible to plan ahead.

Some purchases, such as school lunches, are fixed and absolute necessities. If your weekly spending money includes money for lunches, that money should be spent on lunches—even if you occasionally think you'd rather do something else. If your spending money includes any pre-allocated sums, whether for lunch money or anything else, be sure to set that money aside, either mentally or in actual fact, at the beginning of the week. Don't include it, even wishfully, in your discretionary income, the amounts you are deciding how to spend.

Your actual discretionary money, the decision-making money we have been talking about, is the amount you have on hand to spend after fixed expenses are taken care of. This is the money you will want to think about. It's fine, for example, to spend it all in an afternoon at the bowling alley—as long as you realize, before you do so, that you will have nothing left for other purposes. It's equally fine to spend it all on afternoon snacks, as long as you see that that is where the money goes. A little thought in advance forestalls that sinking feeling many people get when they realize that the money is gone—and an important purchase remains to be made. You can stay in control if you consciously make your spending decisions; don't let them happen by accident.

BUDGETS

"It's no fun, and much too much trouble, to make out all those charts and everything. Budgeting is for bookkeepers."

You may think so too. But budgeting is actually a tool to help you make financial decisions, to keep you in control of your financial affairs. A budget, even one kept only temporarily, can help make dreams come true, help you reach long-term goals. A budget is a guide to help you get the most satisfaction from your money. Without a budget, you may decide how you'd like to spend your money and then find that the decision is a sand castle, washed away by the tide. You might think of a budget, therefore, as a road map; following it will help get you where you want to go.

Budgets don't have to be boring. And they don't

have to be rigid and inflexible. You want a budget that will, as simply as possible, help you keep track of where your money goes and help you to have money available for future needs. You can do this in a number of ways, depending, in part, on your purpose.

Most people who keep budgets do so in order to be sure that they have money available when they need it. A budget designed for this purpose is a budget that measures both income and outgo in advance, both the money you expect to receive in a given time period and the money you expect to spend in that same time.

A written budget. You can keep this kind of budget on paper. (See illustration, p. 11.) First, jot down all the money you expect to receive in a given period of time, perhaps a week or a month, from every source. Think about all your sources of income—allowance, earnings, gifts—but don't count on any "maybe's." Grandma may have given you cash for a birthday present last year, but find the perfect gift this year instead. Then, make a list of all the things you can think of that you spend money on. Put the items in categories. Movies and bowling, for example, might come under the heading of entertainment. New stamps for your collection might be listed under hobbies.

Then, take a large sheet of paper or a notebook, and list projected expenses for the same period of time. Think about immediate expenses and long-term expenses, both this week's movie and next month's hol-

A WRITTEN BUDGET

	WEEK OF			
INCOME	*Jan. 3*	*Jan. 10*	*Jan. 17*	*Jan. 24*
Allowance				
Baby-sitting money				
Presents (*I still have some holiday money!*)				
TOTAL				
OUTGO				
Lunch at school				
Club dues				
Snacks				
Hobby supplies (*more glue?*)				
Entertainment (*movies? bowling?*)				
Saving				
For dad's Feb. birthday				
For school trip				
TOTAL				

iday presents. And divide your expenses into those which are fixed, over which you have no choice, such as lunch money or club dues, and those which are optional, such as a snack or a movie.

A calendar may come in handy for long-term planning. Look ahead at school vacations. Do you spend more money or less when you're on vacation? Either way, if you know when the vacations are, you can plan ahead. Figure out when all the family's birthdays fall. If you are lucky, they'll be spread throughout the year; if you're not, they may be bunched in a short period of time and you may have some extra-careful planning to do to be able to buy all the gifts you want to buy. Knowing this in advance, however, makes planning possible.

Writing everything down is not the end of your budget, however; it is only the beginning. If your projected outgo exceeds your anticipated income, you will have to trim expenses. The place to do that is in your optional list. You may be able to postpone the purchase of a new record or, if necessary, do without it altogether at a time when your other expenses are heavy. It takes some self-discipline, but if your budget shows that you will run out of money without it, the discipline is well worth it. Otherwise, the record may provide temporary pleasure and long-range frustration.

A *"backwards" budget* may work too. Here you think first in terms of what you would *like* to have, then make the budget fit your desires. Instead of first allocating immediate expenses, in other words, and saving what's left for long-range goals, look ahead; plan for long-range goals first. If a ten-speed bike is your heart's desire, put it at the top of your list. Then figure out everything else you *must* have—and what you can do without to make your dream come true.

Do try to keep some money for day-to-day pleasures, however; don't save every penny. Otherwise, you may become so unhappy at always doing without, so frustrated at not being able to do things with your friends, that you may go on a sudden spending spree—and wind up with neither a bike nor anything else that really gives you pleasure.

A *"put-aside" budget* is another way to approach advance budgeting; it involves physically setting money aside for specific purposes as you receive it. As soon as you get any money, with this kind of budget, you divide it up; use envelopes, or jars marching across your desk or dresser, according to the purposes for which you intend to use the money. You might have one envelope labeled "lunch money" and another labeled "baseball bat," depending on your needs and goals. Then, the most important thing—and the hardest—is to keep your hands off the money until the particular purpose comes along. Reminding yourself that you set your own goals may make it easier.

Whichever form of pre-planning budget you adopt, of course, allow yourself some flexibility. Always try to keep some money aside for the spur-of-the-moment fun things that come along. Don't allocate money so rigidly that you miss out on last-minute opportunities. Be prepared to change your budget as your needs and interests change. And don't worry if your budget doesn't balance right away, if your income doesn't seem to match your outgo. Keep at it. Practice will help make perfect.

A *"see-where-it-went" budget* is an after-the-fact budget. If your money seems to disappear without a trace, and your goal in budgeting is simply to see where all your money goes, you want an after-it's-spent record. Carry a small notebook or pad of paper around with you for a month and make a record of every single purchase, no matter how small—every stick of gum, every candy bar, every soda. Be honest with yourself. Don't leave anything out.

If you want to be methodical, you can put the sums down in categories: food, entertainment, records, sporting goods, hobbies, and so on. But a simple day-by-day account of your cash outlays will serve the purpose of this kind of budget: to help you see how money dribbles away so that you know where it goes. You may, after keeping track for a couple of weeks, be shocked to see that most of your money has been spent in the local candy store. You may decide there are better things to do with your cash. Or you may be satisfied. Either way, you'll have a clear picture of where the money actually goes and, if you are unhappy about it, you can do something about it—such as staying out of the candy store and away from temptation.

This kind of budget can be a short-term operation,

just long enough to make the picture clear. It's not the kind of budget you would keep over months or years. Once you've seen where your money goes, you're back in control.

FEELINGS ABOUT MONEY

"I think shopping is fun. I like to buy things, and I like to spend time in stores, even if I don't buy anything. I don't understand Nancy; she never wants to spend any money."

How do you feel about money?

How do you feel about the things money can buy?

How do you feel about going shopping, about the process of spending money?

Many things affect the answers to these questions: the mood you're in, your basic personality, your past experiences with money, what your parents say about money, and what they do.

People, old and young, have moods, and moods can affect the way we act when we spend money. If things aren't going right, for example, if we don't feel particularly good about ourselves, sometimes a new toy or gadget will lift the mood. But if we're very down about something, if everything seems to be going wrong, sometimes we can't seem to make a decision about which item to buy.

If we are happy when we go shopping, on the other hand, feeling good about ourselves and about the world, we may enjoy just looking and not feel the need to buy. Or, if we are happy, we may buy something frivolous, something silly that we don't really need, and feel very good about it because it's fun.

Temporary moods, of course, shift up and down. But basic personality patterns affect spending too. Are you an extrovert? an outgoing person who likes to be with people, to try new things, to taste new foods? Then, chances are, you spend money fairly freely. You may occasionally make impulsive purchase decisions, which you sometimes regret, but you aren't likely to hoard money, to tuck it away and never enjoy the pleasure it can bring. Psychologists say that this is because secure people, people who basically are confident about themselves, can spend money comfortably. They don't feel, inside, that they have to hold on to money for the security it brings.

Insecure people, however, people who seldom feel sure of themselves, are frequently also unsure about spending money. When people are afraid to make a mistake, afraid that they will be criticized if they do, it sometimes seems easier not to make a decision at all. It may seem better to hold on to the money itself. But there are no hard-and-fast rules about human behavior. Some insecure people, instead of holding on to their money, find a great deal of pleasure in buying things for themselves. Possessions seem to bestow confidence.

A person who doesn't feel comfortable with other people may turn to collecting "things" as a substitute. This is a pattern it is better to break. Collections are fun, possessions are fine . . . but not *instead* of friends. Collections can be a springboard for making new friends. If you like to collect soda bottle tops or coins or seashells or picture postcards or almost anything at all, there are others interested in the same thing. All you have to do is find them: look at hobby magazines, talk to your town recreation department or community center about starting a club, put a notice up on your school bulletin board. Enjoy your collection alone, and share it with others as well.

Security and insecurity can be relative too. They should not be considered permanent personality traits when you are still in your teens. In fact, your security/insecurity feelings may resemble a yo-yo. Don't worry about it: *all* young people (and older ones too) feel insecure sometimes. It takes time to become sure of who you are.

Some differences in personality, doctors have found, are evident right from the beginning, right from birth. Some babies in the hospital nursery are very calm and placid. Others are strong-willed and independent. The differences show up at feeding time. The placid babies wait for dinner and eat quietly when it arrives. The strong-willed infants cry lustily and thrash around when they are hungry; they eat vigorously too. Ask your mother what you were like as a baby. But remember that infant behavior is only a clue to later behavior, not a pattern you are obliged to follow.

Your personality and the way you behave is also shaped by your family and by the experiences you have as you grow up. You probably have heard your parents talking about money. You may have overheard an occasional disagreement about money. Because money is so important in our lives, because it permits us to live in comfort when we have it and creates misery when it is absent, money—and the things we do with money—generates strong feelings in people. If mother gets a raise in salary, for instance, you may hear a discussion about what should be done with the money: should it be used to paint the house? buy a new car? Or should it be banked, perhaps, toward next summer's vacation or to pay for your future education?

Because your parents are two different people with different personalities who come from different families, their feelings about money may sometimes conflict. Your mother may have been brought up to believe that it is wise to save as much money as possible, to have a financial reserve for emergencies; she may want to bank her increased salary. Your father, however, may come from a family in which his parents didn't worry too much about the future; he may feel that the money can safely be spent. The positions may be reversed and your father may advocate saving and your mother spending.

Either way, you may overhear some heated conversations. It doesn't mean that your parents no longer love each other, or that they don't love you; it simply reflects the fact that decisions have to be made, that there are always different things that can be done with a given amount of money, and that two individuals do not always agree. In fact, a single individual sometimes has difficulty deciding what to do; if you live with one parent, you probably also realize that decisions aren't easy.

Even when people agree that money must be spent on a particular purchase, there can be disagreements. Suppose your parents have decided to buy a new sofa for the living room. One parent may feel that it would be wise to buy an expensive sofa, with upholstery of fine quality, because it will last longer and not need to be replaced very soon. The other may feel, with equal justification, that it makes more sense to spend as little as possible because then, when the fabric wears out—as it will—it will cost less to replace the entire sofa. You may hear the same kind of discussion when your parents set out to buy your new winter coat, or ice skates. Both want you to have the best—but may honestly disagree over what the "best" is.

Of course, there are sensible guidelines to follow in making any major purchase; comparison shopping is discussed in the next chapter. But attitudes affect spending patterns too, and your parents are shaped to some extent by *their* basic personality and the way *they* were reared.

Sometimes, too, parents say one thing and seem to

do another. They may tell you to save your money, while they spend their money freely. They may not allow you to buy certain things, but appear to put no limits on their own spending. They may say that money doesn't mean much, but act as if it means a great deal. They may, being human, not even realize the inconsistencies between words and actions.

Whether you want to do things the way your parents do, or think that you may take a different tack when you have your own family, you are influenced by your parents' attitudes toward money. You are also influenced by your friends. But you are your own person, with your own personality and your own ideas. Now, during this period of your life, you are developing your own attitudes and feelings about money.

You may like to shop alone. You may prefer going with friends. You may look upon shopping as a necessary chore. Or you may find it a pleasant way to pass the time. You may feel differently about shopping at different times, and when you shop for different things. Buying a birthday present for your sister may generate different feelings from buying a pair of shoes for yourself; both are very different from helping with the family grocery shopping.

To some extent, your later attitudes toward spending money will be affected by the experiences you have now. Every experience, positive or negative, is valuable. If you've bought something and then regretted if, if you've been scolded for "wasting" money on something or other, if you've bought something that has given you great pleasure, if you've enjoyed buying presents for others . . . all of these experiences contribute to your feelings about money itself and about the things you can do with money.

YOUR MONEY'S WORTH

"That neat shirt didn't fit at all after I washed it once. I don't think it would fit a Barbie doll."

Money is important. But money has no value in and of itself. It is only important because we can exchange it for goods and services. It has value, therefore, in terms of the things we exchange it for. It has convenience, because it is easier to carry money to exchange for a desired item than to carry along an item of equivalent value. You may trade, or barter, occasionally, swapping comic books or games with a friend. But, for most transactions, money is more useful than the barter system.

Money also has a fixed value, a value that everyone understands. When you swap, there can be an honest disagreement over values: Is one new Superman comic worth one or two Archie comics? With money, there is no such confusion.

Specific value, however, in terms of what you get for your money, can change. It can change in two ways—as a result of general inflation in the nation's economy and as a result of your own personal buying practices. During times of inflation, prices rise and your dollars buy less; it takes more money to buy the same thing. You may have heard someone say that a dollar is only worth forty-seven cents; what they're saying is that a dollar today is buying what forty-seven cents could buy several years ago.

Inflation affects everything we buy: clothing and toys and records and food. Bubble gum, for instance, could be bought for one penny apiece for many years; as the costs of making and distributing it rose, however, bubble gum manufacturers finally had to raise the price. It went to two cents apiece in 1974, a 100 percent increase. You may have no more money in your pocket, so, if you want to buy bubble gum at its increased price, you can buy fewer pieces. There is very little you can do about the buying power lost through inflation other than, perhaps, negotiating a larger allowance or earning more money on your own. Allowances and earnings will be discussed in later chapters.

But you do have control in another area, because the value of money also shifts with the degree of buying wisdom you bring to the marketplace. Money has more or less value, in other words, in terms of what you choose to do with it. The more you get for your money, by smart shopping, the more value the money has. The less you get, when you make a poor choice or shop impulsively, the less value the money has.

No one is born knowing how to be a good consumer, knowing how to be a smart shopper and get the most value for money spent. It takes considerable practice. You start to get this practice when you first go to the grocery store with your parents. Maybe you pick out some breakfast cereal and your mother suggests that another brand gives more cereal for the same price. Maybe you like plums, but peaches are a better buy that week. Maybe you show your father that one brand of chocolate bits weighs more than a similarly priced package of another brand. Maybe you find that one type of cookie is made of "natural" ingredients, while another contains chemical additives. All of these food-shopping experiences add up to buying wisdom.

As you have more money of your own, and begin to have independent shopping experiences, you have an opportunity to learn still more. You may start out by buying snack food, and discover that one store gives you a larger soda—for the same thirty cents—than the store down the block. You may see that one kind of candy bar is larger than another. As you expand your shopping, as you start to buy more and different things, you will make some mistakes. But don't let mistakes stop you; chances are you'll learn from them and not make the same mistake a second time. If a plastic toy falls apart when it's two days old, you're not likely, after all, to spend your money on the same item again.

You can avoid major mistakes by careful shopping. It's a good idea to know your store, know your product, and know your price.

KNOW YOUR STORE

> *"I bought a record at the shopping mall. Then I saw an ad for the same record on sale, at the local record shop. It's just like throwing away two dollars."*

There are lots of different kinds of stores. They differ in the kinds of goods they carry, the sales and service policies they follow, and the prices they set. A full-service department store, for example, will carry practically all kinds of merchandise: clothing and books and appliances and games and furniture and cosmetics and jewelry. It will sell different types of merchandise in different departments, will have salespeople to wait on customers, and will provide certain services such as delivery and gift wrapping and charge accounts. Prices will vary according to the quality of the merchandise carried by the particular store, but they will have to include enough "markup" to pay for these customer services.

A discount department store, on the other hand, may also carry a large variety of merchandise in a number of departments. But it will offer less service. You may, for instance, have to select your own merchandise from self-service displays and take it to a cashier; if you have a question about the merchandise, you may have trouble finding someone who can give you the answer. You may have to pay extra if you want an item gift wrapped. And you will probably have to carry your packages home yourself because the store won't deliver.

Because the discount store keeps customer services to a minimum, it can also keep its prices down. It is possible, therefore, to buy the same merchandise for less money in a discount store. But don't count on it; always check prices for yourself. Know your merchandise, too. You often must go to a better store for merchandise of better quality. Even where the quality of merchandise, and the individual product itself, is identical, check out the prices on the specific item you want to buy. At times department stores cut their prices on certain items to bring customers in; these are called "loss leaders" because the store will lose money on the particular item but hopes to gain by leading customers to make other purchases once in the store. At times department stores have special sales. Both practices can bring prices down, sometimes to a level below that of the discounter.

Even when prices are higher in a department or specialty store, you may decide to shop there for the service provided. It won't matter for a pair of jeans or a bottle of shampoo. But it might matter on a camera or a radio or a watch. In many cases, such items must be returned to the manufacturer for service. Better stores are more likely to help their customers if a product malfunctions or needs repair. You may also find a better selection of certain goods in specialty shops. The camera store will offer more brands and types of photographic equipment than most department or discount stores, and the salespeople will be more knowledgeable and able to help you make a wise selection.

Department and discount stores, however, are the two major types of stores for most merchandise. They can be found all over the country, in cities and towns and suburban shopping malls. They are convenient when you want a wide selection of merchandise under one roof. But there are a host of other places to shop and, if you are adventuresome, you can discover new ideas and save money at the same time. Variety or dime stores, for instance, offer a wide range of goods at reasonable prices; try a fancy coffee mug for a birthday present, for instance, or pick up an inexpensive tank top or scarf for yourself. Stationery stores are interesting too; a wipe-off memo board or a telephone address book can make a good gift for almost anyone. Hardware and housewares stores often have gadget departments which are fun places to browse for offbeat gifts. And don't overlook charity thrift shops and second-hand stores. They can offer unusual finds in clothing, in books, even in furniture—the perfect shelf, for instance, for your record collection.

Surplus stores and factory outlets are other money-saving shopping spots. In a surplus, or clearance, outlet, a manufacturer or a large store may dispose of merchandise which hasn't sold at regular prices. Sears Roebuck, for instance, has surplus stores for catalogue merchandise where toys and bicycles and clothing are sold at rock-bottom prices. Merchandise stocks change rapidly in such outlets, and you may have to return frequently to find just what you are looking for.

A retail store should be called a factory outlet only when it is actually located at the factory where the merchandise is produced. Real bargains can often be found on items sold at such locations. They may be of first quality, the result of overproduction, or they may be less than perfect; examine carefully before buying. There are factory outlet stores in almost any area where there are factories; they may not advertise widely, however, and you may have to ask around or call the factories in which you are interested to find out whether they will sell to the public.

Another good bet, for outdoor equipment and rugged clothing, is the Army-Navy Store. If you like jeans and parkas and work boots, this kind of store can be a fashion center for you. Prices may or may not be bargains, but chances are you may not find the same items elsewhere.

Wherever you shop, know the store's policy. Can you return an item if it proves defective? If so, can you get your money back? Or must you accept a credit slip and take the amount in other merchandise? There are no laws requiring merchants to take back merchandise or to give you a refund; it's strictly up to the store. Your best protection is to know before you shop. And, although some stores will take things back just because you've changed your mind, it really isn't fair to make a habit of this; it only drives prices up too, as the store must pay for the paperwork and salesclerk time involved. Try to make up your mind while you're in the store, and only buy the item if you're sure it's right for you.

Within a particular store, you can save money by shopping in the right department. If you're small for your age, for example, don't stand on ceremony: buy in the children's department instead of the junior miss or the student department. Sometimes you can buy the very same shirt or sweater for a couple of dollars less. Sometimes the large "boy's" shirt is exactly the same size and style as the small "student's" shirt, in fact, but costs less. There's more status in saving enough money to buy an extra item than in shopping in a department with an older-sounding name. Look for gifts in the notions department, too, or the kitchenware or bath or card shop, rather than in a department labeled "gifts." You may find interesting and useful items at moderate prices.

KNOW YOUR PRODUCT

> *"My new camera broke the first time I used it. The shutter jammed. It's supposed to be guaranteed, but the store said they can't fix it. I have to pack it carefully and mail it to the factory. That costs money. And I won't have the camera when we go on vacation."*

Before you go to the store, you probably have some idea of what you plan to buy. You may want the same game your friend has, or one that you've seen advertised on television. You know by now that advertisements, because they are designed to make merchandise look good enough to buy, play up the good points and play down any disadvantages. An advertisement may not be intentionally dishonest. But the game that looks bigger than life on the small screen of the television set may look disappointingly small when you get to the store. While advertising can bring worthwhile products to your attention, you have to judge for yourself before making a purchase.

Evaluate a product carefully. Look at it. Is it well made, or does it look as if it will fall apart very soon? Does a toy have sharp edges or brittle pieces that are likely to break? Does a game have all the necessary pieces? Is what's inside the box as big and exciting as you might expect it to be from the picture on the cover? Will you—or an adult—have to put the thing together before it can be used? Read descriptive labels before you buy. They often provide valuable information about use and care. The directions on a new game should be clear and easy to follow, not puzzling and frustrating. Instructions on mechanical equipment should be precise.

In clothing, the law now requires that a sewn-in tag indicate what the fabric is and how it should be cared for. Some materials have to be dry-cleaned, others can be washed. Some, like the popular Indian cottons, should be washed by hand in cool water to avoid shrinkage; others, including permanent press and wash-and-wear blends, can be thrown in the washing machine and automatic dryer. You may not have to personally care for your own clothes, but, if you want to get the most for your money, it pays to read and understand the care instructions. Your clothes will last longer and look better if they are properly cared for. Look at the clothing construction carefully too: Is there a hem? Are seams wide and well sewn, with small stitches, so the garment won't separate at the seams after one wearing?

Better construction is usually found in more expensive clothes, but it may not always pay to make the investment. If you are growing quickly, or if the clothing is a fad item that may only be popular for a short time, cheaper is probably wiser. Look for solid construction in a winter jacket that you will wear to school every single day; don't worry about it as much in a T-shirt, but be prepared to re-sew the seams after a washing or two.

In some items, store brands represent a good purchase. Many supermarkets, for instance, have their own brand labels, not only on food but on cosmetics and toys. Big department stores, too, frequently put their own name on certain products. These "house brand" items often sell for less than the comparable item with a national brand label. The items may be very similar, but the national brand has to be priced high enough to cover the cost of national advertising and distribution. Check out the private brands; see if they suit you. Remember that a more expensive product is not necessarily a better product.

If you have saved your money to buy a camera or a typewriter or a watch or a radio, an expensive item with working parts that can malfunction, you will want to know something about the manufacturer as well as about the store in which you buy. Do your homework. Go to the library and look at one of the impartial consumer magazines that compare and rate products; they will indicate which brand or brands has the best features, lasts longest, and gives the least trouble. Then go to several stores and look at the products for yourself; see which one has the features that you particularly want and falls within your price range. Here, too, you may find private brands, frequently produced by major manufacturers for large store chains, at lower prices.

The most important thing to check in any major purchase of this sort is the manufacturer guarantee or warranty. It takes some careful reading of the small print, but it's worth your while to know the guarantee before you buy. Is the entire product, or only part of it, guaranteed against manufacturing defects? For how long? If a part needs replacing, is the cost of the labor included under the guarantee? Or will you have to pay for it separately? What do you do if your watch stops running, or your radio fails? Do you take it back to the store where you purchased it? to a service center run by the manufacturer? Or do you have to mail it back to the factory? What will it cost you, in money and in aggravation, to have the product repaired?

The answers to these questions can help you decide which of two comparable products to buy. If, for instance, manufacturer A has a regional service center right in your town, while manufacturer B requires that you mail your defective radio back to the factory several hundred miles away, and pay the mailing costs yourself, which purchase, all other things being equal, makes more sense? The time to decide, of course, is before you buy. Don't rely on the spoken promises of a salesman; read the written label on the product itself. As of January 1, 1977, federal law requires that a warranty, when one has been issued, be clear and specific—and available for reading before purchase. Once you make your purchase, fulfill your end of the bargain by mailing back any required registration card and by taking care of the product in accordance with instructions.

KNOW YOUR PRICE

> *"I saved up $10 to buy a work shirt. Then I found out they cost $14. And I forgot all about sales tax. I was so mad that I blew the $10 on records. Now if I want a shirt I have to start saving all over again."*

Just as you usually have some idea of what you intend to purchase before you get to the store, so you should have some idea of how much you intend to spend. Consult your budget to determine your limits, and find out what things cost, before you actually go shopping.

One way to determine costs is to read: read newspaper advertisements, read mail-order catalogues. Go window-shopping. Then start to visit the stores. Look for the item you want in different types of stores. A particular popular record, for example, may be available in department and discount store record departments as well as in the local record shop. The discount store may have a regular policy of lower prices on records; the department store or the record shop may be having a special sale. When you plan to buy an advertised special, cut out the ad and take it with you; that way you'll be sure of the price and so will the salesclerk.

Legitimate sales offer excellent opportunities to save money. Reputable stores have sales for many reasons. Sometimes one item is marked down to draw customers into the store; the person who comes to buy a reduced-price record, the theory goes, may also buy another record or clothing or cosmetics at the full price. Sometimes stores overestimate the demand for a particular item; when it doesn't sell, it will be reduced in price to make room for new merchandise. Sometimes merchandise has seasonal ties and must be sold before there is no demand for it at all.

Summer clothes, for example, go on sale in early July so that the stores can make room for new fall styles; if you buy your shorts or bathing suit on sale right after the Fourth of July, you'll still get two full months of wear, and at savings of close to 50 percent. Similarly, ski clothes and equipment will go on sale before the end of the ski season. Toys are frequently marked down in price after the Christmas buying season is over. A good rule of thumb is to think about when the peak demand for an item will occur, then try to buy just after the peak has passed; choices may be a bit more limited, but the savings are well worth while.

Not all sales, unfortunately, are legitimate, and not all stores are reputable; the wise consumer is wary. Compare prices before you shop; then you will know the usual price and won't be taken in by a large sign that screams SALE!!! and actually lists a higher-than-usual price. Don't be pressured by salespeople, either. You have the right to look at merchandise (but not to abuse it) and then decide not to buy anything. You also have the right to buy at the advertised price, and not be talked into a higher-priced item. The Better Business Bureaus call this the "bait-and-switch" game. The "bait" is an ad for a product—a record player, perhaps, or a TV set—at a ridiculously low price. The "switch" takes place when the fish, you, takes the bait and comes to the store; the salesclerk tells you that the advertised item is really not a good buy: for just a "few more dollars" you can have, he claims, a much better item. Don't do it. Leave the store.

Stores also should not be "all out" of advertised sale merchandise. If they really are temporarily out of stock, they should willingly give you a rain check so that you can buy the item later at the sale price. If limited quantities of seasonal merchandise are reduced in price, however, stores may indicate in the advertisement that quantities are limited; then, when the merchandise is sold, it is sold, and no rain checks will be issued.

It helps, too, if you know the jargon of the marketplace. If an item is marked "regularly sold at . . ." the price should be the one at which the item was last sold. If the ticket says "originally . . ." then the item may have been reduced in price one or more times. "List price" means a price suggested by the manufacturer; the item may or may not ever have sold at that price. "Special purchase" means that the store purchased this merchandise especially for this sale; it may never have sold at a higher price. And "going out of business" should mean exactly that: that a store is closing and reducing its prices in order to sell off its remaining merchandise. Many towns license businesses that are actually going out of business, and the license must be displayed during the sale. When this is not the case, some less-than-honest businessmen may run stores that are constantly "going out of business"—largely in an effort to make casual buyers think that prices are a bargain. Needless to say, they are no such thing.

The wise shopper can save money even when the stores are not having sales. You may be able to buy "irregulars" or "seconds" on some items, either in a regular department or discount store or in a store specializing in such merchandise. In every large manufacturing operation there will be an occasional mistake. If the mistake is a minor one, and the resulting defect won't affect wear, the item may be sold as an "irregular"; such a garment might have uneven stitching or an almost invisible discoloration. If the defect is more significant and may affect wear, the item must be labeled as a "second."

Both irregulars and seconds can be good buys . . . if you know what you are buying and examine the merchandise carefully. If you plan to cover your brand-new jeans with decorative patches, for instance, it won't matter to you if the color is streaked. If you are handy with a needle, it may not matter that the seam of a shirt is split. But always be sure to examine every inch of merchandise that is labeled either irregular or a second.

Mail-order buying is another possibility, but it presents a unique set of problems for the unwary consumer. Merchandise may be ordered by mail from local department stores, from large companies that specialize in mail-order selling, and from small outfits that often feature gadgets and novelty items. Local department stores, which you can visit, may run ads in your local newspaper inviting orders by mail; in this case, if you order by mail, you know the reputation of the store and whether or not it stands behind its products and provides customer service. Major national companies specializing in mail order, such as Sears Roebuck, Montgomery Ward, and J. C. Penney, also have reputations they are eager to maintain, and, if merchandise is defective in any way, you can count on prompt and courteous service.

The big problems lurk in the area of small companies that sell only by mail, companies that may be reachable only through a post-office box in some far-off town. You may come across their ads in comic books or magazines. "Send for . . . postage stamps, miniature dolls, face creams, nail hardeners. . . ." Many of these companies are honest and will send you what you order. But be sure you understand exactly what you are ordering. Don't rely on a picture alone; read the description carefully—and be sure it is complete. The size of the item, for instance, should be clearly spelled out in the advertisement or in the catalogue; if it is not, and you order anyway, you may be disappointed when your order arrives. Look for a guaranteed delivery date in the ad, and for the company's policy on returns. Be sure you understand the costs, too; a "free sample" for which you are asked to send $1.98 is not altogether free. Find out whether you are responsible for postage and handling costs, and what those costs will be. And see, if you can, whether the same merchandise is available in your local stores; you may still prefer to order by mail, but you will have a clearer idea of what you are getting.

If you do order by mail, be sure that you send the company all the information necessary to fill your order: your full name and address, including zip code, as well as the price and particulars of the product you want. If you won't accept a substitute item in your order, say so. And don't send cash through the mails. It can easily get lost, and you will have no record of your order. Ask an adult to write a check for you, or buy a postal money order; that way the money can travel safely, and you will have a receipt.

Allow plenty of time for delivery. Don't wait until Thanksgiving has passed to order Christmas gifts. But know your rights as a consumer. The Federal Trade

Commission, because so many mail-order companies used to take months and months to send merchandise, now requires that companies state, in the advertisement, what the shipping period will be; if they don't say, they have thirty days to ship your order. If there will be a delay, the company must notify you and ask your approval.

If the merchandise has not been shipped within the advertised time, or within thirty days, you are entitled to get your money back. Keep track of the time. And keep a record of your order—what you ordered, when, and how much money you sent. Keep a copy of the original advertisement. Then, if the merchandise is greatly delayed, write to the company with all the details.

If delays mount up so that the merchandise, when it finally arrives, is of no use to you—if dad's birthday is in August and the fishing rod you ordered arrives in October, after you finally bought him another gift—you may refuse the package. Don't open it. Just write on it "Refused—Return to Sender." Don't add any postage; the sender will pay the cost. Then write a letter to the company, to be sent separately, explaining why you have refused the merchandise.

If you have opened a mail-order package and discovered something wrong, you will have to rewrap it and pay the postage to send it back. Most companies will refund the postage, however, if the merchandise must be returned because of company error.

Not all mail-order merchants, unfortunately, are

honest. Some take your money and never deliver the merchandise. You can bring such companies to the attention of consumer agencies (see the next section), but you may or may not get your money back. Some companies send the merchandise but have made exaggerated claims about what their products can do. If the claims are so exaggerated that they constitute what is called "false representation," the United States Postal Service may step in and prevent the company from using the mails. It takes a while for such action to be taken, however, so it is up to you, as a consumer, to do two things: (1) Examine advertising claims carefully and decide if they are realistic before sending your money; if an offer sounds too good to be true, it probably is. And (2), if a company does prove to have misrepresented what its product can do, tell the Postal Service about it; ask your local post office for the appropriate form.

Still other companies send unsolicited merchandise and ask for money. If you receive anything in the mail that you haven't ordered, a box of greeting cards or a bar of soap or a packet of stamps or anything else, federal law says that you may consider it a free gift. You do not have to pay any bills that the company sends.

When you sign up for a mail-order book or record club, however, you agree to what is called the "negative option" way of doing business. That means that the club sends you its selections automatically, and bills you for the purchase, unless you advise the club that you do not want that month's selection. The Federal Trade Commission does require, though, that the club give you at least ten days in which to reply. The FTC also requires that membership terms be clearly spelled out; you should know in advance, for example, whether or not you must buy a specified number of items in a given period of time.

When you sign up for a book or record club or a series of magazines, you are signing a contract. Always read such an agreement carefully before signing it, and *never* sign a contract which contains blank spaces; keep a copy of the contract too. If you agree to a contract presented at your home by a door-to-door salesman, you have seventy-two hours in which to change your mind. After that the contract is legally binding. There is no such mind-changing leeway on other contracts; think it through before you sign.

Book and record clubs are generally honest enterprises. But they may not represent any saving to you. Compare their prices with local retail prices before you sign up. And know what your commitment is: After the big money-saving introductory offer, how many books or records will you be obliged to buy? How many of these would you have wanted to buy if you were not a club member? Find out, too, if the books or records or tapes are the editions you want. You may not mind receiving a book in different covers from the bookstore version, not if the words are the same; you may mind very much receiving a favorite song in an unfamiliar arrangement. With book and record clubs, as with any other purchase, know what you are buying.

One other fact about ordering by mail: Once you order, even once, you will probably find yourself getting a lot of mail. Companies sell lists of mail-order customers to each other, and your name and address will find their way from one company to another. Order one magazine subscription, send away for one package of magic tricks, and you will receive endless bids from other companies seeking your business. Some of this mail can be fun to read, some of it can be a nuisance. If you don't like getting so much mail, or if some of it is distasteful to you, there is a way to make much, if not all, of it stop: Write to the Mail Preference Service, Direct Mail/Marketing Association, 6 East 43rd Street, New York, New York 10017 and request the form that will remove your name from the mailing lists of their 1,800 member firms. You will still get mail from organizations that do not belong to DM/MA; it is impossible to stop the flow completely, but you may be able to reduce it to a trickle. You may also request the U.S. Postal Service to stop delivering objectionable mail.

If, however, you would like to be put *on* mailing lists, would like to receive information about certain kinds of products, you may write to the Direct Mail/Marketing Association's Mail Preference Service and ask for its "add-on form." This form contains a list of subjects from which you can choose, including automobiles, books and magazines, records, stamp collecting, and so on; it also has an All Subjects category. You may change your mind at any time and, by writing to the DM/MA again, request that your name be removed from either the name-removal or add-on file.

Some mail-order merchants do not sell products at all; at least they say they don't. Watch out for:

- The "awards" distributor. He offers to include you in a directory of "outstanding" students, or to provide you with a scroll commemorating your "accomplishment" in some area. The catch: The awards have a price. Legitimate honors and listings in legitimate directories are free.
- The "job" merchant. He advertises "get rich quick" and "earn big money in your spare time" schemes. The catch: He asks you, first, to pay for expensive working materials. Don't get involved in any such arrangement without careful investigation.

Consumer protection agencies can sometimes come to your aid if you have difficulties with either local or mail-order merchants. If you have an honest-to-goodness complaint about a product—not if you've simply changed your mind and don't want it—your first course of action is to complain to the seller. Don't yell, don't scream, don't exaggerate; just describe the problem clearly and accurately. Be specific. Know all your facts: when you bought the item, how much it cost, what the problem is. On any major item, such as a camera or a watch, you should always keep your sales receipt and the manufacturer warranty that comes in the box.

When your complaint concerns a local retail store, ask for the customer service department in a department store or the manager in a small local shop; there's little point in complaining to a salesclerk. If the store won't help, won't fix or replace an item that has failed to function properly, your next step is to write directly to the manufacturer. Again, include all the facts. But don't send the original and only copy of your receipt; send a photographic copy.

If your problem is with a mail-order company, check to see if the company has a toll-free customer service telephone number; many large companies do. If not, write to the customer service department or the company president. If the company does not reply to your complaint within thirty days—keep a copy of your letter and all supporting documents—write to the Mail Order Action Line, Direct Mail/Marketing Association, 6 East 43rd Street, New York, New York 10017, and they will try to help.

If your problem—with either a local store or a mail-order concern—remains unsolved, your next step is to turn to consumer protection agencies. On store-bought items, contact your local Better Business Bureau or your state office or department of consumer affairs or your state attorney general. On mail-order merchandise, write (include a copy of the advertisement if you can) to Director, Bureau of Consumer

Protection, Federal Trade Commission, Washington, D.C. 20580. These agencies will try to help. But your best protection, always, is to be a wise shopper; investigate before you buy.

SHOPLIFTING

"I only took a record. A big store like this won't miss it."

Not so. Big stores do miss small items. And more and more stores are doing something about the rising tide of shoplifting. They are arresting shoplifters, even (sometimes especially) juvenile shoplifters. They are pressing charges against them. They are making sure that criminal records stick.

Is it worth it? Is it worth it to break up the boredom of a summer afternoon? Is it worth it to take a dare? Is it worth it to get attention?

There was a time, in folklore if not in fact, when shoplifting was a "prank." That time, if it ever existed, is long since past. Shoplifting is a multibillion-dollar crime in the United States these days, not a prank but a crime. Shoplifting costs you money. Every time you buy something—food or clothing or records—the cost of that item reflects the cost of what merchants call "shrinkage." Shrinkage is the disappearance of merchandise through thefts of all kinds, including shoplifting. Contrary to what you may think, big businesses are not faceless corporations made up of money; they are actually, in the case of retail stores especially, people trying to make a living on a very small profit margin. When that margin is decreased through theft, prices must be raised. But prices can't go up too much, not without losing business. So merchants are trying to reduce theft. One way they are doing this is by pressing criminal charges against shoplifters.

Young people picked up for shoplifting often think they will be let go because they are young. Instead, many stores are trying to deter shoplifters by "making an example" of them. That means, often, your name and address in the local newspaper. It means, if you are caught and prosecuted, an excellent chance for a criminal record. Such a record can keep you out of college and prevent you from entering certain careers. If you decide at the age of twenty-one that you want to go to law school, and you were picked up at fourteen for pocketing some cosmetics in the dime store, you may just have to forget about becoming a lawyer. Just being arrested, even if you are later found innocent, can create long-range problems. If you have to fill out a job application form which includes the question "Have you ever been arrested?" do you think you will get the job?

Your chances of being picked up are excellent. Stores are watching you closely. They use mirrors, cameras, and detectives. The "teen-ager" in jeans next to you at the record counter may be working for the store. If you slip a record under your jacket, she will notice. Don't do it.

CREDIT

"My mother uses credit cards all the time. It must be great to shop without money."

Maybe you've used credit too. Have you had lunch at the local pizza place, under an agreement that your mother would pay for it later? That's a form of credit. Have you borrowed your mother's department store charge card, together with a signed note of authorization, and gone shopping? That's a form of credit. Have you had your teeth cleaned and then seen your father, the following month, write out a check to the dentist? That's a form of credit too.

Credit, simply speaking, allows people to use goods and services before paying for them. Instead of doing without while saving money to pay for needed or wanted items, the credit user enjoys the items immediately and pays for them later. The use of credit is increasingly popular and increasingly widespread.

But credit has disadvantages as well as advantages. True, it's nice to have the use of something while you're paying for it . . . but will the something last as long as the payments do? True, credit is convenient; it's nice to shop without having to carry large sums of money . . . but that same convenience can lead to temptation, to dangerous impulse buying beyond the ability to pay.

Many people, of all ages, have found the easy availability of credit dangerously tempting. Such people often find themselves in deep financial trouble before they realize it, as they owe more money than they can possibly repay. This kind of money problem has broken up young marriages, and older ones too.

But credit is with us to stay. And it can be a useful tool, as long as users understand what it can and cannot do. Whether or not you are ready to join the large numbers of American teen-agers who are already using credit in some form, it's a good idea to understand what it is all about.

TYPES OF CREDIT

Credit includes such things as consumer loans from banks, installment purchases of automobiles and furniture, and mortgage loans on houses. Few of these are likely to concern you, at least for a while.

The most common form of credit, the form with which you may already be familiar, is the charge account. A charge account is a formal agreement between a merchant and a consumer, an agreement that the merchant will give the consumer a product or service on the promise that it will be paid for at a later date. If the payment will not be made right away, as soon as the bill is presented, the agreement will usually also include an additional sum, a service charge or interest fee for the privilege of delaying payment. An agreement with the local pizza place, that your lunches will be paid for, may not be in writing; it may be based on an understanding between the store owner and your parents. Similarly, the dentist's understanding that bills will be sent the following month for services performed, and that the bills will be paid promptly, is based on custom. The department store charge account, however, is a legal agreement based on a formal written application.

You may have seen advertisements for American Express or Diners Club cards, or seen adults paying bills this way; these, and others like them, are called "Travel and Entertainment," or T & E, cards. The customer pays a fee, somewhere between $15 and $25 a year, for the privilege of having one of these cards. With the card a wide variety of goods and services can be charged, everything from meals in restaurants to overnight stays in hotels. These cards are designed primarily for business people and are not available to teen-agers.

Bank cards, such as Master Charge and the Visa card, also are usable in many places and for many things, from neighborhood boutiques to travel agencies. The cards have been free, except when the customer is late in paying, but some banks are now beginning to charge a monthly service fee. These cards are also not readily available to young people.

The retail charge account will probably be your personal introduction to the world of credit. Such charge accounts are issued to valued customers by merchants, whether small neighborhood stores or large shopping center department stores; the card is good only in the store of the issuing merchant. Sometimes special teen-age accounts are offered, with limited amounts of credit—perhaps $30 to $50. Small jewelers sometimes offer these accounts, encouraging teens to buy friendship rings and identification bracelets for themselves or as gifts.

You may have such a teen account or, perhaps, a regular department store account in your own name. Or you may be allowed to use an account in the name of one of your parents. Either way, you are responsible for paying the bills you run up. It may seem easier to let your parents do so, if they are willing, but it's a good way to get into long-range credit difficulties. Many people who face financial difficulties as adults point out that they did not learn to handle money responsibly as young people. Paying bills is part of responsibility; don't charge items unless you can pay for them.

There is generally no specific fee imposed for the use of the retail charge card. But that does not mean that credit is free.

THE COST OF CREDIT

If you think about it, credit has to cost money. The merchant does not get his money right away, even though he gives you the product or service. He also has to maintain records about the purchase, much more complicated records than are necessary with a simple cash transaction. He has to pay a staff to maintain those records.

Merchants can make back the cost of credit in two ways: through a direct charge to the credit customer, or through raising prices for everybody. Either way, the store that extends credit has to charge for it. This is why you will sometimes (but not always) find that stores which do *not* offer such customer services as charge accounts may have lower prices.

There may also be specific charges associated with the use of credit. You will find many variations on retail charge accounts, but there are basically two types: the "regular," or "30-day," account, in which there is no interest charge if bills are paid within the 30 days; and the "revolving," or "open-end," account, in which you have the choice between paying in full and paying no interest or delaying payments, up to a previously set purchase limit, at a previously agreed upon rate of interest.

The regular account is very much like paying with

cash, since you must pay almost immediately, but it does have the advantage of allowing you to pay a single bill for all purchases at that store within the month. And it allows you to shop without carrying large amounts of cash. The revolving account offers more flexibility; if you pay right away, it acts like a regular account, and if you pay a portion of the balance each month, it is like an installment purchase or time payment plan.

If you delay paying in full, however, by paying a portion of the balance each month, you must pay a surcharge or fee for the privilege. One percent, or one and a half percent, per month may not seem like much, but it is important to calculate the actual cost. At 1½ percent per month, true interest charges are 18 percent per year. That's enough to cancel out any saving you may have thought you were getting by buying in a hurry.

Whenever you are tempted to use credit, stop and think: will the amount by which the stereo set, or the winter coat, is reduced on sale be a real saving after I add on interest charges to pay for it through a charge account? Or would I be better off putting my savings in the bank, where they will earn interest, until I have enough to buy what I want? Most items do go on sale periodically, too, so you can have it both ways: earn interest on your savings and then buy in cash. Avoid buying on credit just because it is easy; be sure the things you buy are things you need and need right away. There certainly are times when an immediate purchase makes sense, even if it means paying added interest charges. If the item is something you will enjoy long after you finish paying for it, if it is really a good buy, and if you will have the discipline to make your payments as they come due, then it may be worthwhile to buy on credit. But use only as much credit as you can comfortably repay. Go back to your budget and plan your use of credit in terms of anticipated real future income. Don't live beyond your means.

Whenever you do buy on credit, you are entitled to know exactly what you are paying. Federal Truth in Lending laws require that both *finance charges* and *annual percentage rate* be clearly spelled out. The finance charge is a dollar amount, the actual dollars-and-cents cost of obtaining credit. The annual percentage rate allows you to compare credit costs regardless of the dollar amount of the costs or the amount of time in which payments are made. Interest costs can be tricky. Look at this example from the Federal Reserve System:

> Let's suppose you borrow $100 for one year and pay 6 percent—or $6—for that money. If you have use of the entire amount for one year, you are paying an *annual percentage rate* of 6 percent. But if you repay the $106 in 12 equal monthly installments, you do not have use of the entire amount for the full year. In fact, over the entire year you have the use on the average of only about half the full $100. So the $6 charge for credit in this case becomes an *annual percentage rate* of 11 percent.

Some stores charge interest on the amount which is actually unpaid, others on the average balance remaining in the account during the month. It is important to know, before you make a credit purchase, just what the cost will be.

ESTABLISHING CREDIT

Once you have decided that it is worthwhile to make use of credit, you will have to make an application with the particular store. Stores grant credit to customers who show that they *can* repay and that they *will* repay. The *can* comes from your source of income, allowance or earnings. The *will* comes from your demonstrated character, your previous credit record if you have any, and references from adults who know you well. There has to be a first time, before you have any previous credit record, and it helps, for example, if you have a bank account in which you have made regular deposits. You can, whether or not you have an established credit record, expect the credit officer of the particular store to ask a lot of questions—after all, the store will be, in effect, loaning you money, and they have a right to know if they can expect you to repay the loan. Then, after all the questions have been asked and answered, you will be asked to sign the credit agreement. It is a contract; read it carefully before you sign.

If you have not yet established a credit record of your own, you may be asked to secure your parent's signature on your application—and your parents, too, have the right to expect that you will be responsible for paying your bills.

YOUR RESPONSIBILITY

Once you have opened a charge account, you are responsible for paying your bills promptly. Don't take the matter lightly and say, "I'm short of cash this month but it's a big store; it can wait." It is your responsibility, in accordance with the credit agreement you have signed, to pay your bills. If, in a real emergency, you find it absolutely impossible to pay promptly, write a letter to the store explaining the situation. Most stores will be reasonable, once notified. If you do nothing, however, the store will probably file a credit bureau report which says that you do not pay your bills. Such a report can haunt you in later years. Credit bureaus share information on a national basis. If your file contains a notation that you are a bad credit risk, you could find it difficult, for years and years to come, to establish credit. Your credit record should be considered permanent; do not think that, because you are a teen-ager, you will not be held responsible for paying your bills.

Stores do occasionally make mistakes. Keep your receipts and sales slips so that you can match them against your statement when it arrives. That is especially important today because many stores, in their switch to computerized billing, no longer send out copies of the sales slips. Instead, the statement probably contains a department number which will give you a clue as to where you made a purchase three weeks earlier; it will make things easier for you, however, if you keep your bills all together and know exactly what you bought and when.

Your monthly statement will also include a billing date and a date when payment is due. If you have a revolving account, it will indicate your new total balance and the minimum payment due if you want to stretch your payments out; if you pay less than the total due, the statement will also indicate the interest rate and finance charge. Some stores have a minimum charge of fifty cents.

If you do find an error on your bill, there are two things to do: First, if the amount in question is small, pay your bill. Second, outline your complaint in a separate letter mailed directly to the customer service department; do not include your complaint on or with the bill itself.

If you pay the bill, you will forestall additional finance charges while the matter is being straightened out. Then, if the charge is in error, your account will be credited with the proper amount. If you are overbilled by a substantial amount, however, you may be unable or unwilling to make the payment. The federal Truth in Lending Act protects you in such cases; it prevents the store from taking any action against you while a complaint is being resolved. But it is up to you, under the act, to notify the store promptly and in writing with the details of your complaint. The act also requires that every creditor spell out in writing its procedures for resolving billing errors; you will find this information on the back of the bill or on a separate sheet enclosed with each monthly billing. Meanwhile, during resolution of a billing problem, you do have to pay other portions of your bill.

Keep close track of your credit cards; they are valuable. Be sure you get your card back after you make a purchase. And keep a list, somewhere at home, of your cards and their numbers. Then, if one should be lost or stolen, you can notify the store right away. The law now states that you are not responsible for the total bill someone may run up on a card he finds or steals. But you are responsible for $50 worth—a healthy sum—unless you notify the company immediately. If you find a credit card missing, therefore, first call the store to report the loss and then put the notification in writing. The same is true with any other kind of credit card.

LAYAWAY PLANS

Layaway is not credit, but it is often confused with credit. With a purchase on credit, you receive the merchandise before you pay for it. With a layaway, the merchant puts the merchandise aside for you until you finish paying. This can be a legitimate way of doing business, helping you to acquire items you could not otherwise afford. But it also, according to the Better Business Bureaus, lends itself to abuses.

When you give a store a deposit, therefore, and ask them to hold merchandise for you:

• Do business with a reputable store, not one that will put pressure on you.
• Be very sure you really want the merchandise—and will still want it when you finish paying for it.
• Be sure you will be able to pay for the merchandise—and be sure you understand how much time you have to do so. The time allowed is not established by law, but is purely a matter of store policy.
• Be sure you understand the terms of the layaway plan. Will you get your deposit back if you do not finish paying for the item? If not, can you apply it to other merchandise? Or will you simply lose the money? The terms should be spelled out in writing on the layaway receipt. Keep the receipt.
• Watch out for hidden charges. There should be no interest or finance charges on a layaway plan.

SAVING

"My folks are always talking about rainy days. Why should I worry about saving when it may never rain?"

You, too, may have been urged to save some money "for a rainy day." But what is a rainy day? And what does it have to do with money?

Putting money aside for rainy days started out as saving some money just in case an emergency developed; money on hand to pay doctors' bills in case of sudden illness serves the same purpose as a handy umbrella in case of rain.

People still talk about rainy days, but the meaning has broadened to include many kinds of future need, not only true emergencies but major expenses which can be anticipated: a new car, a paint job for the whole house, higher education.

In addition, as people realize that small amounts of money saved on a regular basis add up to substantial sums, other saving goals come into being. The family with a little extra cash, instead of dribbling it away week by week, can put it aside for luxuries too big for current income, for the optional extras that make life fun. Depending on the interests and goals of the particular individual or family, such savings might be directed toward a color TV or a stereo, a sailboat or a trip, or a host of other things.

Young people, too, can save their money for bigger things, for long-range buying pleasure. You may have first realized the power of saving when you had your eye on a big package of plastic cowboys. Or maybe it was a super-size yo-yo, or a glow-in-the-dark Frisbee. Whatever it was, the money in your pocket was not enough. Rather than give you more upon request, however, mother or dad suggested that you save part of your money each week until you could buy the thing you wanted. You weren't so sure, at first, but you tried it, and it worked.

Now you know the power of saving. But knowing doesn't make it easy. If you are saving for some particular purpose, a camera or a bicycle or a youth hostel trip or whatever, try putting aside a portion of your income each week, designating it for that purpose *before* you do any small-scale discretionary spending. Before you go to the movies, in other words, or buy an ice-cream soda, put aside the amount you've determined to save. It makes it a lot easier.

You can put the money aside at home, in an envelope or an old wallet or an empty peanut-butter jar. But when you have more than a few dollars put aside, and more than a few days or weeks in which to save, why not put your money to work?

Putting money to work means putting it in the bank, in an interest-earning savings account. Money is working when it's in use, and money is kept in use when it is deposited in a savings account. Banks use the money deposited by their customers to loan to other people; the money in your account may be helping your uncle to buy a new car. Because banks use your money this way and charge your uncle for the use of the money he borrows to buy his car, they also pay you, the depositor, for the privilege of using your money. The money they pay you is called *interest*.

It's easy to be confused by this. Some young people don't like the idea of "their" money being used by other people. But your money is safe in a bank. In fact, most bank accounts are insured by the federal government so that, even if something should happen to the bank (which is very unlikely), you would still get your money back. Some children also think that they should get back the "same" money they have put into the bank. Depositors do get the same *amount*, but the bills and coins, which have been kept in use, are not necessarily the same bills and coins. You may deposit five one-dollar bills and, when you make a withdrawal, receive a single five-dollar bill; the amount, of course, is the same. The money itself may be different because it has been out working, not sitting still and waiting for you. Remember that, by letting your money be used, you are earning more money through interest.

KINDS OF BANKS

Your first experience with banking may have been with a school savings plan. If your school has such a plan, you could bring some change with you to school once a week and deposit it in your account.

Perhaps your initial experience with banking was a trip to the local bank with your mother or father. You may have just been along on errand day when a stop was made at the bank to cash a check or make a deposit. Or perhaps a special trip was made to deposit a birthday check you had received from a relative.

You may not have realized it then, but there are several different kinds of banks. Commercial banks, sometimes called full-service banks, offer a whole range of banking services, including both checking and savings accounts; because they offer more services than any other type of banking institution, they usually do not pay quite as much interest on savings accounts. Mutual savings banks and savings and loan associations are both primarily savings institutions; they have some financial services, such as making loans when people want to buy houses, but they do not generally offer checking accounts. Savings banks and associations usually pay slightly more interest on savings accounts.

The amount of interest which any financial institution may offer is limited by the federal government. Commercial banks have not been allowed to pay as much as savings institutions. Some individual institutions, however, will offer the allowed maximum; others will offer less.

CHOOSING A BANK

You will want a bank that pays the most interest, but you will also want a bank that wants to have you as its customer. That means that the bank will have convenient banking hours, in the late afternoon and/or on weekends, so that you can do your banking when you are not in school. It also means that the bank will accept very small deposits and will keep your account active even if you have only a few dollars in it. A very big bank, one that does a lot of business with stores and corporations, may not be particularly interested in a customer who deposits two or three dollars at a time; a smaller neighborhood bank may be very happy to have you as a customer. They know that as you get older you will have larger sums to deposit.

The amount of interest, however, and the way in which it is credited, remain important. The way in which interest is credited varies enormously and is so complicated that very few adults understand just how it is done. The simplest way to put it, however, is to explain the two factors that go into figuring interest: when it is compounded and when it is paid.

All banks *compound* interest; they pay interest on

interest left on deposit. Simple interest, by contrast, would be interest paid only on the original sum deposited. You earn more when interest is compounded. If your $30 in the bank, for instance, has earned thirty-two cents in interest at the end of the first interest period, the next interest calculation will be made on the basis of $30.32. And so on.

The more often interest is compounded, the more often the amount on which the interest is paid is calculated, the more money you can earn. The best bet, therefore, is a bank that does its compounding of interest on a daily basis. Banks compound interest at different time intervals, however—daily, monthly, even quarterly (four times a year); you will have to ask.

Banks also differ in their policies about crediting interest to depositors' accounts. Some pay interest on the basis of how much is actually in the account on the first day of the month. Others allow a "grace period" of ten days at the beginning of the month, in which amounts deposited will earn interest back to the first. And some pay interest on the average amount in the account during the month. The best possible arrangement for you, as a depositor, is usually a "day of deposit to day of withdrawal" account. In this arrangement you can earn interest on your money for exactly as long as it is on deposit.

Interest is credited on different dates too: the first of the month and the end of the quarter are frequently used dates. It's important to know what your bank does, and then be sure that you don't lose interest by taking money out of your account just before the day on which interest is credited.

Find out, too, how much you must have on deposit before you will begin to earn interest. A bank may be willing to open an account for $10, but not pay any interest on amounts under $25. Others will pay interest on small sums. You should find out in advance.

Once you start to put your money to work, just a few dollars a week adds up to substantial sums over a year or more. If you put $5 a week in a piggy bank, for example, you would have $260 at the end of a year and $520, or exactly twice as much, at the end of two years. The same $5 a week at 5 percent compound interest, however, gives you $266.45 at the end of one year and $546.48 at the end of two. That's equivalent to several extra weeks of saving.

Look at this example of the power of compound interest, provided by the American Bankers Association:

> In 1791 Benjamin Franklin left $5,000 to the citizens of Boston, on the condition that it be allowed to accumulate for one hundred years. By 1891 the fund had grown to $322,000. After a school was built and paid for, $92,000 was set aside for a second hundred years. In 1960, this fund had reached $1,400,000.

Few of us put our money aside for so long, but it's easy to understand why Franklin wrote, "Money makes money and the money that money makes makes more money."

WHAT KIND OF ACCOUNT?

Now that you're all excited about saving, and you've picked the bank in which you'll save, what kind of account will you have?

Your parents may be putting money away for you. If they are, they are probably using either a trust account or a custodial account. In either case, the money isn't really yours and you can't touch it—at least not until you've reached legal age.

Now that you're ready to save some money of your own, however, you do want to be able to put your hands on the money. That's an important point: money can come out of a bank account as well as go into it. If you choose to put your money to work in a bank account, don't look upon it as a permanent and irrevocable decision. Remember, you're saving for a purpose. When you have enough to buy that ten-speed bicycle or to take that trip you've been dreaming about, that's the time to make a withdrawal.

In order to be able to do so, you want an individual account in your own name. Most banks will allow you to open an individual savings account as soon as you are old enough to sign your name in script. Some, however, insist on a minimum age of twelve or, sometimes, fourteen, for individual savings accounts. If your bank does that, you have two choices: Ask a parent to open a joint account with you, in which case either of you has the same right to make deposits or withdrawals. Or find another bank.

Another form of individual account, one you

should know about, is the "club" account. These are savings accounts—the most popular is the Christmas Club—in which you agree to make a deposit of a fixed amount each week. You then get the money back at a specified time; in a Christmas Club it would be just in time to do your Christmas shopping. Club accounts, in many banks, pay no interest at all; in some they pay interest, but at a lower rate than a regular savings account. Their main attraction is that they are a form of forced saving. If you can stick to a saving plan on your own, you are much better off with a regular account.

Whatever form of account you open, keep it active. Even if you don't make any deposits or withdrawals for several months, be sure to present your savings bank book (if you have a passbook account) at the bank to have interest credited. If you don't do this, the bank may think you've moved away. Then, if they can't find you after a period of years—exactly how long depends on the state—your money is given to the state government. Don't let that happen.

HOW TO OPEN AN ACCOUNT

When you're ready to open your savings account, ask to see one of the officers of the bank; their desks are usually located right out in the open on the banking floor. You will be asked to fill out a signature card. Then, when you put money in or take money out of your account, your signature will be matched against the signature on file. This protects your money. Since your signature may change as you grow older, however, it's a good idea to fill out a new signature card every once in a while; when you try out a fancy new signature, or when you suddenly notice how much your handwriting has changed since you were in the fifth grade, that's a good time to bring the bank records up to date.

Many banks have "passbook" accounts in which you are issued a savings account book. Every time you make a deposit or a withdrawal, under this type of account, you must present the passbook together with the appropriate form. Your deposit or withdrawal, together with any interest due, is noted in the passbook and your current balance is entered. With this kind of account, you should present your passbook every once in a while to have the interest noted, even if you are not making a deposit or withdrawal. It is also very important to keep the passbook in a safe place.

Other banks today have what are called "statement" savings accounts. With this type of account, you do not have a passbook. Instead, the bank sends out a statement, often every three months, showing your deposits, withdrawals, and earned interest.

CHECKING ACCOUNTS

Checking accounts, offered by full-service commercial banks, are a convenience for people who have many bills to pay. You may have seen your parents writing checks for the monthly rent or mortgage payment, for the telephone bill or for a department store purchase. When people use checks to pay bills, they do not have to carry large amounts of cash, or send money through the mail. Checks are not just pieces of paper, however; they must be backed by enough money in the bank to cover the amount shown. Otherwise, when the landlord or the telephone company or the department store presents the check for payment, the account will be *overdrawn* and the depositor will have to pay a penalty charge.

The only way to know that there is enough money in your bank account to cover all your checks is to keep careful records and to *balance* your account at regular intervals. The first step in careful record-keeping occurs when a check is written: the *stub* in the checkbook must be filled out with the date, the amount, and the payee—the name of the person or company to whom the check is made out. You can also keep track of the purposes for particular checks on the check stub. If you write a check to the Book Nook, for instance, you might jot down that the check was for school supplies; this will serve to jog your memory when you look back at your checkbook later on.

Checks are safer than cash, but they can still be misused. Care should be taken in writing checks so that they cannot be altered: use ink, and write out the dollars-and-cents amount in words. Place both the amount in figures and the amount in words as far to the left as possible so that no one can add a number and increase the amount of your check. Fill in any unused space with a line. Don't write your signature until all the rest of a check is properly filled in. The following diagram shows a properly made-out check:

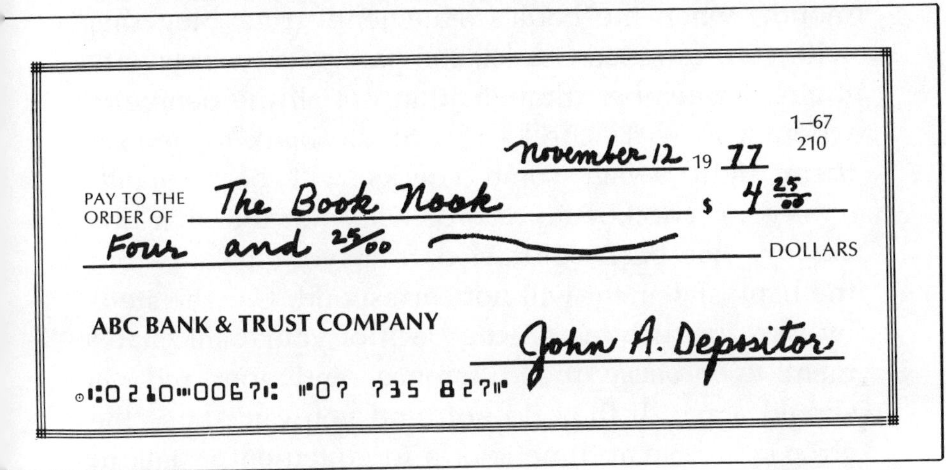

Other safeguards: Use your own checks, and don't allow anyone else to "borrow" a blank check. The odd-looking numbers at the bottom of a check are magnetic characters which identify an individual account; your check, with your identifying number on it, will be drawn against your account—even if someone else signs his or her own name and writes in a different account number. The bank's computers will identify the check only through the magnetic characters and disregard the other information. Keep your blank checks in a safe place and keep canceled checks for several years; they are proof of payment, should you ever need it, and they contain your legal signature, which should be kept out of the hands of potential forgers. If you ever discard a filled-out check, in fact, tear it into little pieces first.

Keep a current balance, a current record of your account, by adding deposits as you make them and subtracting checks as you write them. Then, each month, when the bank's statement arrives, together with your canceled checks, compare your records with theirs. Remember, though, that not all the people to whom you write checks run to the bank to deposit them right away; some checks will be *outstanding*—your checkbook record will indicate that the amount has been subtracted from your balance but the bank statement will not correspond. Use the step-by-step instructions on the back of your bank statement to *reconcile* the difference, and your records should agree. If they do not, and you can't trace the error to simple arithmetic or a forgotten entry, talk to your bank about it. Such disagreements are usually the result of a simple error—but sometimes the error is made by the bank.

Because checking accounts are a convenience for depositors, banks usually do not pay interest on the money kept in them. In fact, banks often charge a certain amount per check for the service. It is not worthwhile to have a checking account, therefore, unless you have many bills to pay. You will probably have no need for one before you graduate from high school.

Meanwhile, before you have a checking account of your own, you may receive birthday and holiday gifts in the form of checks. In order to get the cash which the check represents, or even to put the amount into your savings account, you will have to *endorse* the check. This means that you will have to write your name on the back, across the left side of the check. If you want to cash the check at a bank, you will probably have to have an account at that particular bank; in that case you must endorse the check—write your name—in the form in which your account was opened. If the check is made out differently, write both names: "Joe Jones," and under it "Joseph R. Jones." Don't write your name until you get to the bank, though; once you've endorsed a check it's like cash, and, if you lose it, anyone may try to cash it. If you plan to deposit the check in your savings account, write "For deposit only" before you sign your name and your account number. If you don't have an account but a parent is willing to convert the check into cash, write "Pay to the order of [your parent's full name]," followed by your name as it is written on the check.

INVESTMENTS

Bank accounts are very good places to save money which you may want to use in the relatively near future. With a savings account in a bank, you know that your money is always growing, always earning interest, *and* that it is always available to you.

Sometimes, however, people have extra money to save, money that they don't expect to need for a while. Such money can be invested for a longer period of time. You may have this kind of money if, for example, you have earned a lot at a summer job or if you have been given a substantial gift. The gift may be in the form of money, or it may already have been invested for you.

You may, for example, have United States Government Savings Bonds in your name, bonds bought for you by parents or grandparents. Or you may want to purchase such bonds with your own savings. You can buy a Series E bond for as little as $18.75; after five years it is worth $25—or an interest rate of 6 percent. This is a perfectly safe form of savings because you are lending money to the United States government and the government guarantees that you will be repaid. But, in order to earn the full interest rate, you have to do without the money until the bond matures.

Money may also be invested in securities. Securities include *stocks* sold by corporations and *bonds* sold by corporations and by government bodies.

If you own stock in a corporation, you own a share in that corporation; as a part owner of the business, you share in the profits and the losses of the business. You may earn dividends on stock and you may sell it at any time. Stocks are bought and sold through the Stock Exchange, which operates as a trading center; stock can only be sold when there is someone who wants to buy and can only be bought (except in the case of a new stock offering) when there is someone who wants to sell. Stockbrokers do the buying and selling on the "floor" of the Stock Exchange; they earn commissions, a percentage of the cost, for the work they do. That commission is paid by the buyer and by the seller. Every time you buy or sell shares of stock, the amount of the stockbroker's commission plus taxes on the transaction should be weighed against the possible profit.

If business does well, shareowners can do very well. If business does poorly, shareowners can lose considerable amounts of money. Because stock ownership is so closely tied to the fortunes of business, it is a risky form of investment. Money invested in stocks is not as safe as money put into either a savings account or government savings bonds. On the other hand, if your stock rises in value, you stand to make considerably more money than you could in either banks or bonds. As a general rule of thumb, investment counselors advise that the only money to be invested in the stock market is money that won't be missed too badly if it is lost. You probably won't have money of this kind to invest until after you have finished all your schooling.

Bonds represent money loaned to a corporation or government body. When a road or a school is to be built, for example, a county or town may raise the necessary money through a bond issue. Then the taxing power of the county or town guarantees repayment. When a corporation wishes to expand, perhaps through building a new factory, it too can raise the necessary money by selling bonds. Corporations are obligated to repay bondholders before shareholders; bonds, as a result, are considered a safer investment than stocks. Both corporate and governmental bonds are generally sold in large units, seldom less than

$1,000 apiece, and, although they are not as risky an investment as stocks, they do fluctuate in value.

Chances are that you will not buy stocks or bonds for yourself until you are older. If, however, your parents or grandparents have invested in securities in your behalf—as part of your college fund, for instance—you might find it very interesting to follow the progress of the company in which you are a participant. Ask your parents if you, or they, are shareowners in any particular company. If you are, ask the purchase price of the shares and ask your parents to show you the daily stock quotations in the newspaper, which will show you the current price. Then, if you look at the newspaper from time to time, you can see how the stock shifts in price. You can also relate the daily news to your company. If, for instance, you own stock in a utility company and you see in the newspaper that there might be a shortage of natural gas supplies, what do you think might happen to the value of your stock?

2 WHERE YOUR MONEY COMES FROM

ALLOWANCES

"I get everything I want if I just wait until my dad is in a good mood. I have more money than any of my friends. Why would I want an allowance?"

Does this sound like you? Do you think you come out ahead by not having an allowance? You may, in the short run, actually get more money from your family by not having a regular allowance, a fixed predetermined sum that you get each week. In the long run, however, you would be better off if you could convince your parents that an allowance is a good thing.

Some parents don't give allowances because they think that children spend money too carelessly. Some don't because they think young people, like older ones, should work for what they get. Some believe it is their responsibility, as parents, to approve each purchase made by a child. And still others simply never get around to an allowance; they find it hard to figure just what should go into an allowance, and so they never give one at all. Instead, they take each request as it comes and decide on the spot whether or not to give an okay.

The nice thing about an allowance, though, is that when you have one you can really begin to learn how to manage money. Instead of learning how to manage people—trying to tell, for example, when mom or dad is in a good mood and may say "yes"—you can learn honest-to-goodness lessons about money management.

When you have a regular amount of money, on which you have to get along for a specified period of time, you learn how to make decisions about money. You learn that your decisions are important ones, that a movie may take the place of ice-skating, but that *you* are the one to decide.

With an allowance, you also learn how to take responsibility for your own purchasing decisions. If you have enough money for an ice-cream soda or for a new notebook, but not for both, *you* have to decide what is important—and live with your decisions. You also learn, by making mistakes, that some purchases are wise ones and some are not. An adult may tell you that a particular item is not a good buy, but there's nothing like the personal experience of buying it with your own money to make the lesson real. Once you have bought a toy that has broken in short order, or a shirt that has shrunk, you have learned a great deal about how to shop, and you are not likely to make the same mistake again.

Learning how to manage small amounts of money through a regular weekly allowance is a good way to get the experience which will help you to handle larger sums later on. Once you learn from small mistakes, in other words, you are less likely to make big mistakes. You might use this argument to convince your parents that a regular allowance is the best way for you to learn how to manage money wisely. You might tell them, too, that you won't have to come to them with lots of little—and not-so-little—requests for money if you have regular pocket money to call your own.

HOW MUCH SHOULD AN ALLOWANCE BE?

The biggest stumbling block in many families is deciding just how much children's allowances should be. You want—and your parents want—to settle on an amount that is realistic. Too little money is not good; it will only make you unhappy. And too much money is not good either; if you don't have to make decisions about spending your money, if you don't have to make your money stretch over a period of time, then the allowance, instead of helping you learn about money, will give you entirely the wrong idea.

No one, with the possible exception of a handful of super-millionaires, has enough money to do everything in the world he or she would like to do. And even super-millionaires don't spend their money that freely on luxury items, or they wouldn't be supermillionaires for long. You want an allowance that will teach you how to manage money, teach you how to make the most of what you do have—and that means an allowance in an amount large enough to cover your needs but small enough so that you do have to make decisions about how to spend it wisely and well.

The actual dollars-and-cents amount should be decided by talking things over with your parents. You should not decide all by yourself how much your allowance should be. And your parents should really not decide without consulting you. Sit down together. Tell your parents what you think you would do with an allowance, what you would spend money on in the course of a week, how much you think would be reasonable. Then listen to your parents, to their opinions about whether or not the things you want to do are reasonable, and how much money they are willing to give you to cover the activities of which they approve.

You may have to remind your parents that inflation has made a lot of things you buy much more expensive than they used to be. Comic books can't be had for ten cents any more and neither can candy bars; even bubble gum has doubled in price, while almost any form of entertainment—movies or bowling or ice-skating—consumes significant sums of money. Your parents may very well remind you that "money doesn't grow on trees" or that, as a practical matter, the family income has to stretch much further because of inflation. But if you talk things over calmly, you should be able to reach a meeting of the minds on just how much your allowance should be.

PAY FOR WORK AROUND THE HOUSE

You may think that if you help out around the house you should be paid. Or your parents may suggest that an allowance should be in payment for specific chores.

You should do your part, of course, just because you are a member of the family. As a member of the family, however, you should not expect to be paid for helping the household run smoothly. If your parents choose to give you an allowance (and despite its benefits, no one is "entitled" to an allowance), it should be because they want you to have this opportunity to learn to manage money. Chores—with the possible exception of occasional "special" jobs, paid for separately—should be entirely distinct from the allowance.

WHAT SHOULD THE ALLOWANCE INCLUDE?

Just what an allowance covers is also a ticklish question. Some parents hand out lunch money and call it an allowance. Others make an allowance only "bubble-gum money," money that is not destined for any specific purpose at all. And some provide an allowance which combines ingredients: it may include some fixed sums, like lunch money or club dues or a church donation, plus some "bubble-gum money," the money you can spend as you please.

Both elements of an allowance provide an opportunity for learning about money management. The money you can spend as you please is the money with which you will make decisions. It is the money with which you will make mistakes—and learn from your mistakes. The pre-fixed amounts, however, also serve a purpose. If you handle your lunch money and bus fare and club dues, and make the money last through the week, you are also learning how to handle larger amounts.

Both elements of your allowance should grow along with you. As you move along in school, you will need more spend-as-you-please money, money to keep up with your growing interests and growing circle of friends. As you get older, too, you will be able to handle more of the pre-fixed sums, the sums your parents would otherwise spend on you. By the time you are in high school, for instance, you can probably handle some of your clothing purchases. And you may want to suggest to your parents, at that stage, that you can learn more about budgeting if you receive your allowance every other week or even monthly.

In your family conference, right from the beginning, try to decide just what your allowance covers. Both you and your parents should have a clear understanding of the ground rules before you begin. If your money must stretch to include lunches, you don't want to go hungry during a long school day because you didn't realize that that was the understanding. If your entertainment money must come out of your allowance, you will want to know that too—and put aside some money to go bowling if that's your chosen entertainment for the week. If school supplies are your responsibility, too, you will want to be sure you are properly equipped for school before you go to a movie.

Remember, though, that the first conference should not be the last. Your allowance should be reviewed regularly. In fact, at the beginning, you might want to talk things over with your parents every couple of months. Then, after you've been managing your own finances for a while, once a year might be enough. Many people find that the beginning of each school year is a good time for an annual review.

ASKING FOR MORE

If you find that you simply can't manage, what's the best way to ask your parents for more? Try not to get into the habit of regularly pleading for extra funds; you will only spoil your own chances for really learning how to manage money. Instead, ask for a conference. But come prepared. If you have kept track of exactly where your money has been going, you will be able to present a better case. Don't just say, "I never have any money by the end of the week. I need more." Document your case. Say, for example: "Here is the notebook in which I kept track of everything I spent last month. See, I needed new notebook paper. And I had to replace the strap for my watch. My bicycle tire needed patching. I could only go bowling once all month." If you present a calm, reasonable argument, chances are your parents will listen. They may not be able to meet your request for more money, or they may not think your request is justified, but you will be able to have an adult conversation about the matter.

Your allowance, even though it is very important to you, is only one small part of the total picture of family finances. As you want your parents to listen to you, so you should listen to them. They probably are doing everything possible to stretch the family income to meet a number of pressing needs. They want you to learn about money by managing some, but for a while, if things are tight, you may have to learn by listening. You do, however, have another option: you can earn some money of your own.

EARNINGS

"My next-door neighbor asked me to baby-sit two afternoons a week. I like to take care of Jennifer, and I really can use the money, but my mother said no. She thinks I'll have too much homework this year."

Are you in the same fix? Eager to earn some money but with parents who think you're too busy? Or too young? Or is your problem the other way round? You'd be happy to stick to school and play, but your parents think you ought to earn your own spending money? Or, have you not really considered the matter, just figured that someday you would want a job, but someday is a long way off?

Many young people like to work, enjoy the grown-up feeling of being paid for a job well done. Many like the independence that earned income brings, the freedom from requesting nickels and dimes and dollars from parents every time something special comes along. Many like the experience itself, the sampling of the world of work, and, in some lucky cases, the step along a future career path—or the understanding, equally fortunate, that a chosen career isn't the right one after all.

And many young people do work. More than half of all twelve- and thirteen-year-olds earn at least a dollar or two a week; some earn considerably more. In 1975, according to the Rand Youth Poll, boys from thirteen to fifteen added an average of $4.55 a week to their spending money by working; girls of the same age earned an average of $4.60 a week. The older you get, the easier it is to find jobs, and the more money you are likely to be paid.

Parents frequently have mixed feelings, however, when their children first broach the subject of working. For one thing, it means you're growing up—and much as parents want you to do just that, it can be hard for them to accept, at least at first. For another thing, parents often feel that school comes first. And they're right. Your first commitment at this stage of life is to school, and you want to have enough time to do your schoolwork in the best possible way. You also don't want to be so tired that you rush through your homework, or doze off in class.

If, on the other hand, schoolwork is a breeze and you still have time left over after sports and play and helping around the house, you may be able to handle a part-time job with no problem at all. You may have to provide convincing evidence to your parents, by keeping your school grades up and by remembering your family chores, but if you can do so, they'll probably go along.

In other families, it's the parents who set the stage for children working, either by outright insistence or by keeping spending money to a minimum. In still other families, the question never comes up—until, all of a sudden, there's something you *really* want that you can't get without extra income. Your parents have always been reasonable, but all of a sudden they're not; they refuse to spend the money for a private telephone line or a separate television set or something you consider an absolute necessity, and you realize, after you say, "All right, I'll pay for it myself," that that means getting a job.

When you set out to earn some money, whether the original idea comes from you or from your parents, you face some basic questions. First of all, what can young people do to earn money?

THE JOB MARKET

The old standbys—baby-sitting and lawn chores and newspaper delivery—are still valid today. Many young people, boys and girls alike, do very well at all these tasks as old-time sex barriers crumble. Girls deliver papers and boys baby-sit; girls rake lawns and boys help out at parties. Young people do the jobs they do best—and whatever jobs they find available.

If these jobs all seem to be taken in your neighborhood, however, or if none of them interests you particularly, be creative. Use your imagination and try to see what other jobs need to be done, what service needs to be performed. Neighbors who work full time might like to know that their dog can be walked in the afternoon. Neighbors going on a trip might appreciate having newspapers taken in and plants watered. Mothers often are grateful for help with small children; perhaps you can take a toddler to the playground or run a birthday party for a six-year-old. How about carrying packages? polishing silver? washing up after a dinner party? cleaning out a basement? painting a porch railing? Think of all the things your own parents sometimes need special help with and, after you finish helping out at home, offer your services to your neighbors for pay.

How much should you be paid? That depends on the job and on the amount of time it takes. You would expect to be paid more for moving gardening equipment and cleaning out a messy garage than for walking a dog around the block. People will generally offer you what they are willing to pay, and you are then free to accept or reject the job—or to ask for more. If you are asked how much you charge, however, you have to be prepared with an answer.

For some jobs, like newspaper delivery, there is a fixed rate of pay; for some, like baby-sitting, there is a going rate in the neighborhood. For others, it's up to you. How much would you charge to clean out a goldfish tank? You can charge a flat fee, a set amount, or you can charge by the hour. Either way, try to figure out how long a given job will take and how much effort it involves. How dirty is that goldfish tank and how long will it take you to clean it out? How anxious are you for the job?

In some jobs, experience counts. You might run birthday parties for small children, complete with games and decorations; as you become an expert party-giver, and mothers start to call on you more often, you can charge more for your services. You might make and sell decorated cupcakes; as more and more people ask to buy them, you can increase the price. If you do anything—like selling cupcakes—where you first have to spend money for ingredients, be sure you charge enough to cover your expenses and still make a profit.

Whatever the particular job, however, and whatever the rate of pay, you have an obligation to do it well. Once you agree to perform a certain task for a certain sum of money, your employer will be counting on you. You can't skip walking a dog in order to go off with your friends. You can't disappoint a small child eager to go to the park. You can't leave a lawn unraked if the leaves are piling up and a storm is on its way. You will have to assume the responsibility—if you want to keep your job—of being on time, completing the entire job, and doing it to the best of your ability.

ARE YOUR EARNINGS YOURS TO SPEND?

> *"I've built up practically a full-time lawn-mowing service in the neighborhood. I'm breaking my back this whole summer so I can buy a motorbike—and now my parents say I can't. It's my money, isn't it?"*

Since the initial reason for working, for many young people, is the desire to have spending money independent of parental control, it's sometimes hard to accept that parents still do have control. They do, after all, have the responsibility for your well-being, and if they think that you are too young for a motorbike, you will probably have to live with the decision.

In general, you should be able to use your earnings—just as you should be able to use an allowance—without accounting to your parents for the spending of every penny. On the other hand, the things you choose to do can't conflict with family values, or with parental responsibility for your health and safety. When you disagree with your parents, talk things over calmly; if you can convince them that your reasons are logical and valid, they may change their minds. If they don't, be patient.

As you grow older, in any case, you will realize that long-range pleasures can provide more gratification than short-range ones. When you earn your first few dollars, in other words, you may splurge and buy out the local candy store; when you have been working for a while, you will want to put some money aside for your future. College costs a lot of money; so does any sort of vocational training after high school. When you reach this stage, you will *really* want to be independent. Money—your earnings—can make it possible.

Index

Account. *See* Bank account; Charge account
Advertising, 31, 34–36, 41
Allowances, 10, 24, 57, 81–88
American Bankers Association, 68
American Express card. *See* Credit card
Army-Navy stores. *See* Stores

"Bait-and-switch" game, 36
Bank account
  checking, 71–74
  Christmas Club, 70
  individual, 69
  joint, 69
  passbook, 70–71
Bank account (*continued*)
  statement savings, 71
  trust, 69
Banks
  commercial, 65–66
  savings, 65–66
Better Business Bureau, 45, 60
Bonds, 76–78. *See also* United States Government Savings Bonds
Brands, store, 32
Budget, 9–10, 14, 56, 86
  backward, 12
  "put-aside," 13
  "see where it went," 14–15
  written, 10–11

Charge account, 50, 52–55, 58
regular, 54–55
revolving, 54–55, 58
Checking account. *See* Bank account
Christmas Club. *See* Bank account
Commercial banks. *See* Banks
Comparison shopping, 25, 29, 33, 36, 42–43, 46
Consumer loans, 51
Consumer reports, 33
Credit bureaus, 58
Credit card, 50, 59
American Express, 52
Diners Club, 52
Master Charge, 53
Visa, 53
Customer service department, 45

Department stores. *See* Stores
Diners Club card. *See* Credit card
Direct Mail Marketing Association, 43–45
Discount stores. *See* Stores

Earning money, 10, 24, 57, 89–95

Factory outlets. *See* Stores
Federal Trade Commission, 39–40, 42, 46
Finance charge. *See* Service charge

Guarantees, 33–34

Hardware stores. *See* Stores

Individual account. *See* Bank account
Inflation, 24, 84
Installment purchasing, 51, 55
Interest, 64–68, 75
Irregulars, 37–38

Joint account. *See* Bank account

Layaway plans, 60–61
Loans. *See* Consumer loans

Mail-order buying, 38–45
Master Charge card. *See* Credit card
Mortgages, 51

Passbook account. *See* Bank account

Rand Youth Poll, 90

Sales, 35–37
Savings banks. *See* Banks
Sears Roebuck, 28–29
Second-hand stores. *See* Stores
Service charge, 52, 54–55, 59
Shoplifting, 47–49
Specialty stores. *See* Stores
Statement savings account. *See* Bank account
Stationery stores. *See* Stores
Stock Exchange, The, 76
Stocks, 76–78
Store brands. *See* Brands

Stores
  Army-Navy, 29
  department, 26–28, 35, 37–38, 45, 52–53
  discount, 26–28, 35, 37
  factory outlet, 28–29
  hardware, 28
  second-hand, 28
  specialty, 27–28, 35, 37
  stationery, 28
  surplus, 28
  thrift shop, 28
  variety, 28
Surplus stores. *See* Stores

Thrift shops. *See* Stores
Trust account. *See* Bank account
Truth in Lending laws, 56, 59–60

United States Government Savings Bonds, 76
United States Postal Service, 41, 43

Variety stores. *See* Stores
Visa card. *See* Credit card

Warranties, 33–34, 45

GRACE W. WEINSTEIN has written and lectured widely on money subjects. Her articles have appeared in *Money* magazine, *Parents' Magazine,* and *House Beautiful.* Her book for adults, *Children & Money: A Guide for Parents* (1975), was honored by the American Psychological Foundation.

Mrs. Weinstein was born in New York, graduated from Cornell University, and now lives in Teaneck, New Jersey, with her husband and their two children.